A TAPESTRY OF TALES

A COLLECTION OF SHORT STORIES

AYUSH KUMAR CHHONKAR

Contents

CHAPTER ONE

The Suspicious Town of Millfield

It was a typical summer day in the small town of Millfield. The sun was shining and the birds were singing, but for Emily, something felt off. She couldn't quite put her finger on it, but she had a nagging feeling that something was not right.

She had been living in Millfield for three years, and in that time, she had grown to know and love the town and its residents. But today, something felt different. It was as if everyone was hiding something, and it made her uneasy.

As she walked down the main street, she noticed that the store windows were all shuttered, and the streets were eerily empty. She tried to shake off her feeling of unease, but it continued to linger.

She decided to go to the local cafe to grab a coffee, hoping that a change of scenery would help to clear her mind. But when she got there, she found that it was closed. This was strange, as the cafe was always open during the summer months.

Emily decided to take a walk around the town, to see if she could find any clues to what was going on. As she walked, she noticed that all of the houses had their curtains closed, and there were no signs of life anywhere.

She started to feel a sense of panic rising in her chest. She quickened her pace, trying to make it back to her own house as quickly as possible. But as she turned the corner, she saw something that made her blood run cold.

In front of her was a group of people, all dressed in black and wearing masks. They were standing in front of her house, and they had a large, ominous looking van parked on the street.

Emily froze, her heart pounding in her chest. She knew that she needed to get away, but she couldn't move. Suddenly, one of the masked figures stepped forward and spoke.

"You shouldn't have come back to Millfield, Emily. You should have stayed away."

The voice was familiar, but she couldn't place it. Before she could respond, the figures lunged at her, and everything went black.

When Emily woke up, she found herself in a dimly lit room. She was tied to a chair, and her head was pounding. She tried to remember what had happened, but her memories were foggy.

As she looked around, she saw that she was in a large underground bunker. There were several other people in the room, all of them tied to chairs like her. They were all residents of Millfield, people she knew and trusted.

Suddenly, the door to the bunker opened, and a figure stepped inside. It was the same person who had spoken to her outside of her house. But now, with the mask removed, she recognized him.

It was the town sheriff, a man she had known for years. He had been the one to welcome her to Millfield when she first moved there, and she had always trusted him.

"I'm sorry, Emily," he said, his voice heavy with regret. "But you should have stayed away. We can't let anyone know about what's happening in Millfield. It's for the greater good."

Emily's mind was spinning. She had no idea what was happening, but she knew that it was something sinister. She had to get out of there and warn others before it was too late.

But before she could say anything, the sheriff pulled out a syringe and injected her with a sed.

CHAPTER TWO

Echoes of Loss: A Daughter's Grief

The sun was setting on the small town of Greenwood, casting a warm orange glow over the houses and streets. But for Sarah, the beauty of the evening was lost on her. She was lost in her thoughts, replaying the events of the past few weeks over and over in her mind.

It had all started with the news of her mother's cancer diagnosis. At first, Sarah had been in shock, unable to process the reality of what was happening. But soon, she found herself thrown into a whirlwind of doctor's appointments, treatments, and hospital visits.

Her mother had been her rock, her best friend, and the thought of losing her was unbearable. But despite all the treatments, the cancer seemed to be winning. Sarah watched helplessly as her mother's health slowly deteriorated, until she could no longer even recognize her own daughter.

As the days passed, Sarah found herself becoming more and more isolated. She stopped going to work, stopped seeing friends and even stopped leaving the house. She was consumed by grief and pain, unable to find any solace in the world around her.

One morning, Sarah woke up to find that her mother had passed away during the night. She was alone in the hospital room, holding her mother's hand, tears streaming down her face. She felt a profound sense of loss, knowing that she would never hear her mother's voice again, never feel her embrace.

In the days that followed, Sarah found herself going through the motions of funeral arrangements and receiving condolences from friends and family. But she felt disconnected from it all, as if she was watching it all happen from a distance.

As the weeks went by, Sarah found herself struggling to move on. She was consumed by guilt, feeling that she should have done more, should have been there more. She couldn't shake the feeling that she had let her mother down.

Eventually, Sarah found herself unable to continue with her life as before. She quit her job, sold her house and moved away from Greenwood, unable to bear the memories and pain that the town held.

Years went by, but the memories of her mother and the sense of loss never truly left her. She tried to build a new life for herself, but the weight of her grief always hung heavy on her. She realized that the pain of losing.

CHAPTER THREE

The Last Goodbye

The sun was shining bright on the small town of Oakville, but the warmth and light did nothing to lift the heavy feeling in Emma's heart. She was standing at the edge of the cliff, overlooking the vast ocean, with a picture of her and her best friend, Sophie, in her hand.

Sophie and Emma had been inseparable since they were kids. They had grown up together, shared all their secrets and dreams, and had been each other's rock through the good times and the bad. But now, Sophie was gone, taken too soon by a rare illness, and Emma was left with a void in her heart that she knew would never be filled.

Emma closed her eyes and let the tears flow, remembering all the happy memories she shared with Sophie. She remembered their first kiss under the stars, their first concert together, and all the silly moments they shared. But the memories were also bittersweet as Emma knew that she would never have another moment like that again.

She knew that Sophie would have wanted her to move on, to find happiness and to live her life to the fullest, but Emma couldn't bring herself to do it. She couldn't imagine a future without Sophie, without her laughter and her smile.

For months Emma isolated herself, not wanting to see or talk to anyone, not even her family. She lost her job and her apartment, she stopped taking care of herself, and she let herself fall into a deep depression. She couldn't shake off the feeling of guilt and remorse, feeling that she could have done more to save her best friend, if only she had noticed the signs of her illness earlier.

One day, Emma found herself standing at the same cliff where she and Sophie used to come to watch the sunset. She remembered how Sophie used to tell her that this was the most beautiful place on earth, and that they would always be together, no matter what. Emma knew that Sophie was right, they would always be together in her heart.

She took a deep breath, and with a heavy heart, she let go of the picture and watched it fly away with the wind. It was her last goodbye to her best friend, and Emma knew that it was time to let go, to move on and to start living again.

But the grief and guilt never truly left her, and Emma struggled to find happiness in her life, she couldn't shake off the feeling of emptiness and loneliness, knowing that a piece of her was missing forever. The pain of losing Sophie was too much for Emma to bear, and it became a constant companion throughout her life.

It was a sad ending for Emma, a reminder that sometimes, no matter how much we love and care for someone, it's not enough to keep them by our side. Grief is a powerful and long-lasting emotion, and it can change a person's life forever.

The Unfinished Symphony

The rain was pouring down heavily on the city of New Haven, but inside the concert hall, all was calm and quiet. The stage was set, the musicians were tuning their instruments, and the audience was eagerly waiting for the performance to begin.

The symphony orchestra was about to play one of the most challenging and beautiful compositions of all time, Beethoven's Symphony No. 9. This was a once in a lifetime opportunity for the musicians, and for the audience, it was a chance to experience something truly extraordinary.

As the conductor stepped onto the stage, the audience erupted in applause. He raised his baton, and the musicians began to play. The opening notes of the symphony filled the concert hall, and the audience was immediately transported to another world.

The music was powerful, emotional, and profound. Each musician played with precision and passion, and the result was an orchestral masterpiece. The audience was captivated, and as the symphony progressed, it was clear that this was something truly special.

The second movement of the symphony was particularly moving. The cellos and basses played a melody that was both sorrowful and hopeful, evoking feelings of loss and longing. The audience was spellbound, and many were in tears by the time the movement came to an end.

As the symphony entered the final movement, the tension in the concert hall was palpable. The choral section was about to sing the famous "Ode to Joy," and everyone knew that this was the moment that would make or break the performance.

The choir began to sing, and the audience was overwhelmed by the beauty of the music and the message of unity and brotherhood. The symphony reached its crescendo, and the audience was on their feet, cheering and applauding.

But as the final notes faded away, the audience realized that something was wrong. The symphony had ended prematurely, the last movement was incomplete. The conductor looked confused and the musicians were shocked.

As the audience sat back down in their seats, the conductor stepped forward to explain. He revealed that the symphony was missing the last movement, it had been lost for centuries, and despite the efforts of scholars and musicians, it had never been found.

The audience was in disbelief, they had just witnessed something.

CHAPTER FIVE

A Life Half Lived

The sun was shining brightly on the small town of Willowdale, but for Jane, the warmth and light did nothing to lift the heavy feeling in her heart. She was sitting on the porch of her childhood home, surrounded by memories and regrets.

Jane had always dreamed of leaving Willowdale and seeing the world, but she had never found the courage to do so. She had stayed in her hometown, living a life of routine and safety, never taking risks or pursuing her passions.

As the years passed, Jane watched as her friends and family moved away, following their dreams and building fulfilling lives for themselves. But she remained stuck in the same place, watching the world pass her by.

Jane knew that she had missed out on so much, that she had let her fears and doubts hold her back. She realized that she had spent her life playing it safe, never truly living.

As she sat on the porch, she thought about all the opportunities she had missed, the adventures she had never taken, and the love that had never been pursued. She felt a deep sense of sadness and regret, knowing that she would never be able to go back and change the past.

In her later years, Jane became increasingly isolated, with little human contact, she was consumed by her regrets and missed opportunities. She realized that she had wasted her life and that it was too late to make any changes.

On her deathbed, Jane was surrounded by her memories, but no loved ones, she knew that she would be leaving this world with nothing but regrets, a life half-lived. She closed her eyes for the last time, knowing that she had missed out on so much, and that her time had run out.

It was a sad ending for Jane, a reminder that life is short, and that we must make the most of every moment. We must be brave, take risks, and follow our dreams, because we never know when our time will be up.

CHAPTER SIX

Heels Up

The sun was setting on the city of New York, casting a warm orange glow over the skyscrapers and the busy streets. But for Samantha, the beauty of the evening was lost on her. She was sitting on the edge of her bed, staring at the pair of red heels on the floor in front of her.

Samantha had always been a career-driven woman, working hard and climbing the corporate ladder. She had sacrificed a lot to get to where she was, including her personal life, and she had always put her career first.

But now, she had finally reached the top, and she was the CEO of a successful company. She had everything she had ever wanted, the money, the power, and the respect. But as she sat there, staring at the heels on the floor, she realized that something was missing.

She thought about the long nights she had spent working, the missed dinners, the cancelled plans. She thought about the people she had hurt and the relationships she had sacrificed. And she realized that she had traded it all for a pair of red heels.

Samantha felt a deep sense of emptiness and loneliness, knowing that she had given up so much for a job that didn't fulfill her. She realized that she had been chasing the wrong things all along, and that she had lost herself in the process.

It was then that Samantha made a decision, she was going to leave her job and start living her life. She was going to travel, see the world, and find herself. She was going to put her heels up and start living.

She quit her job, sold her apartment and left her old life behind. She traveled to different countries and met new people, she discovered new cultures, food, and languages. She fell in love, and got her heart broken. She had some of the best moments of her life and some of the worst. But most importantly, she found herself.

Years went by, and Samantha returned to the city, but this time as a different person. She had a newfound appreciation for life, and she knew that it was too short to be wasted on anything that doesn't make you happy. She started a new company, one that was focused on empowering women and helping them find their true selves.

Samantha had finally found her happiness, and it had nothing to do with the pair of red heels she had left behind. It was about the journey she had taken, and the person she had become. She had finally put her heels up and started living.

CHAPTER SEVEN

The Vanishing Act: A Suspicious Story

The night was dark and stormy as the small town of Ravenswood was gripped by fear and uncertainty. A local businessman, Jack Williams, had gone missing without a trace, leaving behind his wife and children, and a community in shock.

Detective Samantha Green was assigned to the case and immediately set out to investigate. She interviewed friends, family, and associates of the missing man, but no one had seen or heard from him. The only lead was a mysterious phone call that Jack had received the night before he disappeared.

As the days turned into weeks and the investigation hit a dead-end, the case started to gain attention from the media and the public. The pressure was on, and the detective had to find answers.

Samantha soon discovered that Jack had a secret life, one that involved illegal activities and a dangerous group of associates. It seemed that he had gotten himself into a dangerous situation, and his disappearance could be connected to his illicit activities.

As the evidence piled up, the case took a sinister turn, and it became clear that someone had a motive to harm Jack. The detective and her team worked tirelessly to uncover the truth, but the culprit was always one step ahead.

Just when it seemed that the case was going cold, a break came through. A witness came forward and reported seeing Jack at a secluded cabin on the outskirts of town, on the night he disappeared.

Samantha and her team raced to the cabin, but what they found was unsettling. There was no sign of Jack, but the cabin was cleaned and tidied, as if no one had been there for a long time. The detective and her team searched the area but found nothing, it was as if Jack had vanished into thin air.

The investigation was closed, and the case was never solved. The community was left with more questions than answers and the fate of Jack Williams remains a mystery. The detective was left with a feeling of unease, as she couldn't shake off the feeling that something was off, that something was being kept from her.

The story of Jack Williams became a legend in Ravenswood, a reminder of the dangers that can lurk beneath the surface, of secrets and lies, and of a man who disappeared without a trace. The case remains open, and the truth about what happened to Jack Williams remains a mystery, leaving the ending of this story, suspicious.

CHAPTER EIGHT

The Lost Treasure

The old mansion stood at the top of the hill, overlooking the small village of Blackwood. It had been abandoned for decades, and the villagers avoided it like the plague, believing it to be cursed. But for a group of treasure hunters, the mansion was the key to finding a legendary treasure said to be worth millions of dollars.

The group, led by the experienced treasure hunter, Ethan, had spent months researching and planning their mission. They had uncovered old maps and documents that led them to believe that the treasure was hidden somewhere within the mansion.

As they approached the mansion on a dark and stormy night, the group couldn't help but feel a sense of unease. The mansion was in a state of disrepair, and it seemed to loom over them, watching their every move.

Ethan, however, was determined to push on, and the group made their way inside. The mansion was dark and musty, and it was clear that no one had set foot in it for a long time.

As they began to search the mansion, the group encountered many obstacles, from crumbling staircases to locked doors and hidden passages. But they were determined to find the treasure, and they pushed on.

As they delved deeper into the mansion, they began to uncover clues and hints that led them closer to the treasure. They found old maps and documents that revealed the location of secret rooms and hidden compartments.

The group was getting closer to their goal, but they soon realized that they were not alone in the mansion. They started to hear strange noises and feel a presence following them. They knew that someone, or something, was watching them.

Ethan, however, refused to be deterred, and they pushed on, determined to find the treasure. But as they entered the final room, they were met with a shocking sight. The treasure they had been searching for was not what they had expected.

It was not gold or jewels, but something far more valuable and powerful. They had found a secret laboratory, filled with advanced technology and scientific equipment. They realized that the true treasure was not the gold or jewels, but the knowledge and power that the laboratory held.

As they prepared to leave the mansion, they knew that they had found something that could change the world. But as they made their way out, they were met by a group of heavily armed men, who revealed that they were not the only ones searching for the treasure.

The group was forced to fight for their lives, as the men tried to take the treasure for themselves. But in the end, the group emerged victorious, and they were able to escape with the treasure.

As they made their way back to the village, they knew that they had not only found a treasure, but they had uncovered a secret that could change the world. And they knew that their lives would never be the same again.

The true treasure was not the gold or jewels, but the knowledge and power that the laboratory held, and the group knew that they had to keep it safe, no matter the cost. They had discovered something that could change the world and they were ready to fight to protect it.

CHAPTER NINE

The Endless Quest

The kingdom of Eldrida was in turmoil. The once prosperous land was now plagued by war, poverty, and despair. The people were suffering, and they were in desperate need of a hero.

Enter, Aric, a young and ambitious adventurer, who had always dreamed of making a name for himself and becoming a legend. He had heard of the troubles in Eldrida and knew that this was his chance to prove himself. He set out on a quest to save the kingdom and restore peace to the land.

Aric's journey was long and treacherous. He faced many obstacles and dangers, from treacherous mountains to fierce monsters. But he was determined to succeed, and he pushed on, never giving up.

As he traveled through the kingdom, Aric met many people, some who helped him on his quest, and others who tried to stop him. He encountered knights, wizards, and bandits, and he made many friends and enemies along the way.

Aric's quest led him to the heart of the kingdom, where he found himself face to face with the evil sorcerer, Zoltar. Zoltar was the one behind the war and the suffering in Eldrida, and Aric knew that he had to defeat him if he wanted to save the kingdom.

The battle was fierce, and it seemed that Zoltar was unbeatable. But Aric was not one to give up easily, and he fought on, determined to defeat the sorcerer and save the kingdom.

In the end, Aric emerged victorious, and the kingdom was saved. The people rejoiced, and Aric was hailed as a hero. He had accomplished what no one else had been able to do, and he had saved the kingdom from certain doom.

But Aric's quest did not end there. He knew that there were other kingdoms in need of saving, and other people suffering. He realized that his quest was endless, and he set out to continue his journey, determined to make a difference in the world and become a true legend.

Aric's quest would take him through many lands, facing many challenges and overcoming many obstacles. He would make new friends and allies, and he would discover new powers and abilities. He would become a powerful warrior, a wise leader, and a true hero.

As the years passed, Aric's legend grew, and his name became known throughout the land. He was a hero, a saviour, and a true inspiration to all who knew him. And his quest, his endless quest, would continue forever, as he journeyed through the world, seeking to make a difference and bring peace to the land.

CHAPTER TEN

Last Bells: A Tragic School Story

It was a typical autumn day at Greenfield High School, the leaves were falling, the air was crisp and the students were bustling with excitement. Among them was a young girl named Emily, who was starting her senior year with high hopes and dreams. She was determined to make the most of her last year in high school, and she was looking forward to the new experiences and opportunities that lay ahead.

Emily was a diligent student, who had always worked hard and had a passion for learning. She was a leader in her class, and she was well-liked by her peers and teachers. She had a bright future ahead of her, with plans to attend a top university and pursue a career in medicine.

But as the school year progressed, Emily started to notice a change in herself. She found it harder to focus in class, and she was struggling to keep up with her workload. She was feeling overwhelmed and stressed, and she was losing her passion for learning.

Emily tried to ignore her feelings, and she pushed herself harder, determined to succeed. But the more she tried, the more she realized that something was wrong. She was struggling with depression, and she was unable to cope with the pressure and expectations of her senior year.

Emily's condition worsened, and she started to withdraw from her friends and family. She stopped participating in school activities, and she stopped attending classes. Her grades started to slip, and she was on the brink of failing.

The school administration and her family were worried, and they tried to intervene, but Emily refused to seek help. She felt that she had failed, and that there was no hope for her.

Finally, on a cold, autumn day, Emily couldn't take it anymore. She took her own life, leaving her family, friends and the whole school community in shock and grief. Her death was a tragic reminder of the importance of mental health and the need to reach out for help when it is needed.

The school bell rang for the last time on that day, signaling the end of the school day, but also the end of Emily's life and her dreams. Her classmates and teachers were left with a feeling of emptiness, knowing that they had lost a dear friend, a brilliant student and a shining light in their lives. Her death was a painful reminder of how fragile life can be, and how important it is to reach out to others and seek help when in need.

CHAPTER ELEVEN

The Lonely Writer

There once was a writer named James, who had always been passionate about the written word. He spent his days locked away in his small apartment, pouring his heart and soul into his writing. He had always dreamed of becoming a published author, and of having his work read by the masses.

James had always been a solitary figure, preferring the company of his words to that of other people. He had few friends and no family, and he spent most of his time alone. But he didn't mind, because he had his writing to keep him company.

Years went by, and James's writing began to gain recognition. He received positive reviews, and his work was soon noticed by a publisher. He was offered a book deal, and his dream of becoming a published author was finally coming true.

As his book hit the shelves, James was overjoyed. He had finally achieved his lifelong dream, and he was finally being recognized for his talent. But as the days passed, James realized that his success had come at a cost.

He had been so focused on his writing, that he had neglected everything else in his life. He had no friends or family, and he had no one to share his success with. He realized that his writing had become his only companion, and that he had nothing else in his life.

As the reviews of his book began to pour in, James was filled with a sense of emptiness. He had achieved his dream, but he had nothing else to live for. In the end, he couldn't bear the loneliness any longer, and he took his own life.

His book became a bestseller, but his death was a tragic reminder of the dangers of becoming too consumed by one's passions and neglecting the people and things that truly matter in life. It was a lonely and sad end for a writer who had everything he ever wanted, but nothing he truly needed.

CHAPTER TWELVE

The Anime Enthusiast

There once was a young girl named Mei, who had always been passionate about anime. She had grown up watching her favorite shows and movies, and had always dreamed of becoming an anime creator herself. She spent her days drawing, animating and writing, honing her craft and working towards her goal.

Mei's passion for anime led her to enroll in an animation school, where she studied under some of the most renowned anime creators in the industry. She worked hard, and she quickly gained recognition for her talent. She was determined to make a name for herself in the anime world.

After graduation, Mei landed her first job as an animator at a small studio. She was thrilled, and she was determined to prove herself. She worked tirelessly, pouring her heart and soul into her work. Her dedication paid off, and her animations were well-received by audiences and critics alike.

As her career progressed, Mei began to gain more recognition and respect in the anime industry. She was offered more and more opportunities, and she quickly rose through the ranks. She was soon leading her own projects and creating her own anime series.

Mei's anime series quickly gained a cult following, and it was soon picked up for international distribution. She was thrilled to see her work being enjoyed by audiences all over the world. She had finally achieved her dream, and she was living the life she had always wanted.

But as her success grew, Mei began to realize that the anime industry was not all that it seemed. She saw the harsh realities of the industry, the long hours, the tight deadlines and the constant pressure. She saw the exploitation of young animators and the lack of recognition for their hard work.

Despite her success, Mei couldn't shake off the feeling that something was not right. She knew that she loved creating anime, but she didn't want to be a part of an industry that didn't value its creators. She began to question her own motivations, and she wondered if her passion for anime had blinded her to the truth.

In the end, Mei made the difficult decision to leave the anime industry. She knew that she couldn't continue to be a part of something that didn't align with her values. She wanted to create anime that was true to her and that reflected the world she saw around her.

Mei's story is a reminder that passion and drive can take us to great heights, but it is important to stay true to ourselves and to question the world around us. It's not about the success or the recognition, it's about the reasons why we do what we do and the impact it has on ourselves and the world.

The Code Crusader

There once was a software engineer named Alex, who had always been passionate about coding. He had grown up tinkering with computers, and had always dreamed of turning his hobby into a career. He studied computer science in college, and soon landed his first job as a software developer.

Alex was a natural at coding, and he quickly made a name for himself in the industry. He was a problem-solver, and he was always looking for new and innovative ways to improve his work. He was driven to create the best software possible, and he was always pushing the boundaries of what was possible.

As his career progressed, Alex was offered more and more opportunities. He worked on big projects, and he was soon leading his own teams. He was respected and admired by his peers, and he was on track to become one of the most successful software engineers in the industry.

But as Alex's success grew, he began to realize that something was missing. He was working long hours, and he was always under pressure to deliver. He was never able to switch off, and he was always thinking about work. He realized that he had become a slave to his own success, and that he had lost sight of what was truly important.

Despite his success, Alex felt unfulfilled. He knew that there had to be more to life than just work. He began to question his own motivations, and he wondered if his passion for coding had blinded him to the truth. He knew that he wanted to create the best software possible, but he also wanted to enjoy life and make a real difference in the world.

In the end, Alex made the difficult decision to take a step back from his career. He knew that he needed to find a balance between his work and his personal life. He started to volunteer in his community, and he began to use his skills to help non-profit organizations. He realized that his passion for coding could be used for good, and that he could make a real difference in the world.

Alex's story is a reminder that success is not the only thing that matters. It's important to find balance, and to use our skills and passions to make a real difference in the world. It's about using our talents to make a positive impact, and to create something that is meaningful and lasting.

CHAPTER FOURTEEN

The Lost Love

There once was a young woman named Emily, who had always been in love with her childhood sweetheart, Jack. They had grown up together, and had always been inseparable. They had shared their hopes, dreams and secrets, and they had always known that they were meant to be together.

But as they grew older, their paths began to diverge. Jack was offered a scholarship to study abroad, and he jumped at the opportunity. Emily stayed behind, finishing her studies and working to support herself. They tried to make the long-distance relationship work, but it was hard.

As the months went by, the distance between them grew. They talked less and less, and the once strong connection between them began to fade. Emily tried to hold on, but she knew that something had changed. She knew that Jack had moved on, and that she had lost him.

Emily was devastated. She had lost the love of her life, and she didn't know how to go on. She threw herself into her work, trying to forget about Jack and the life they had once shared. But no matter how hard she tried, she couldn't shake off the feeling of loss.

Years went by, and Emily moved on with her life. She built a successful career, and she found love again. But she could never forget Jack. He was always there, in the back of her mind, a constant reminder of what could have been.

One day, out of the blue, Jack called. He was back in town, and he wanted to see her. Emily was torn. She didn't know if she was ready to see him again, but she knew that she had to. She agreed to meet him, and they met at their old haunt, the park where they had shared so many happy memories.

As they sat on the bench and talked, all the feelings came flooding back. Emily realized that she still loved Jack, and that she would always love him. But she also realized that they could never go back to what they had once been. They had grown and changed, and their love was a thing of the past.

Emily and Jack said their goodbyes, and they knew that it was the end. They hugged and cried, knowing that they had lost something precious, but also knowing that they would always carry that love with them. They parted ways, knowing that they would never forget each other, and that the love they had shared would always be a part of them.

Emily's story is a reminder that love is not always forever, but it is always a part of who we are. It's about learning to let go, and to move on with grace and dignity. It's about holding onto the memories, and cherishing the love that we have shared, because even if it ends, it will always hold a special place in our hearts.

CHAPTER FIFTEEN

The Void's Trapped: A Story of Disappearance and Hope

Once upon a time, in a small village nestled in the heart of the forest, there lived a young girl named Alice. She was known throughout the village for her kind heart and her love of adventure. One day, while wandering through the forest, she stumbled upon a strange, old house that she had never seen before. Intrigued, she approached the door and knocked. To her surprise, the door creaked open and she found herself standing in a dimly lit room.

As she looked around, she noticed that the room was filled with all manner of strange and bizarre objects. There were jars filled with eyeballs, a table made of bones, and a chandelier that seemed to be made of teeth. Despite her initial fear, Alice couldn't help but feel a sense of curiosity and wonder. She decided to explore the house further.

As she ventured deeper into the house, she discovered that it was filled with rooms, each more strange and mysterious than the last. She found a room with a painting that seemed to change before her eyes, and another with a door that led to a never-ending staircase.

Eventually, she came to a room that was unlike any she had seen before. The walls were made of glass and in the center of the room stood a strange, glowing orb. As she approached the orb, she felt a strange pull towards it. Without hesitation, she reached out and touched the orb.

Suddenly, everything went black. When Alice awoke, she found herself in a completely different place. She was no longer in the old house, but in a vast and endless void. She looked around in confusion, trying to make sense of what had happened.

As she looked around, she saw that there were other people in the void with her. They were all people who had disappeared from the village over the years, and they had all been taken to this strange place by the orb.

Alice soon discovered that they were all trapped in the void, and that there was no way out. They spent their days wandering aimlessly, trying to find a way to escape.

Years passed, and Alice grew old and gray. But still, she never gave up hope of finding a way out of the void. One day, she had a strange dream. In the dream, she saw the orb again, but this time, it was different. It was no longer glowing, but instead had a small crack in it.

When she awoke from her dream, she knew what she had to do. She set out in search of the orb, determined to find the crack and break it. After what felt like an eternity, she finally found the orb. And just as she had seen in her dream, there was a small crack in it.

With all her might, she struck the orb with a rock and it shattered into a million pieces. Suddenly, the void began to fade away and Alice found herself back in the forest, in front of the strange old house.

As she looked around, she realized that the house and all its strange contents were gone. And so were all the people from her village who were trapped in the void. They were all gone without a trace. The strange orb that brought them all to the void, also took them away from it.

Alice never spoke of her experience in the void, but she knew that the people of her village were gone forever. And so, she lived the rest of her days alone, but with the knowledge that she had been a part of something truly magical and mysterious.

CHAPTER SIXTEEN

Broken Dreams

It was a bright and sunny day in the small town of Willow Creek. The birds were singing, and the air was filled with the sweet scent of blooming flowers. But for one young girl named Sophia, it was just another day of heartache and sorrow.

Sophia had always been different from the other children in her town. She had a wild imagination and a love for adventure, but her parents never understood her. They wanted her to be a good girl and follow in their footsteps, but Sophia had bigger dreams. She wanted to leave Willow Creek and see the world, to experience all the wonder and magic it had to offer.

One day, Sophia's parents gave her an ultimatum. They told her that if she didn't start behaving and following their rules, they would send her away to a boarding school. Sophia knew that if she went to boarding school, her dreams of adventure would be forever crushed.

Desperate to escape her parents' control, Sophia decided to run away. She packed her bags and set out into the world, determined to make her dreams come true.

For years, Sophia traveled from place to place, experiencing all the world had to offer. She saw beautiful landscapes, met interesting people, and had countless adventures. But despite all her travels, she couldn't shake the feeling of loneliness and homesickness.

As she grew older, Sophia realized that her parents were right all along. She was different and didn't belong anywhere. She was a wanderer with no place to call home.

Sophia returned to Willow Creek, but her parents had passed away, and the house where she grew up was empty. She had nothing left and nowhere to go. She realized that her dream of adventure has turned into a life of isolation and regret. Sophia died alone, a wanderer with no family and no friends.

The end of the story is a reminder that sometimes, chasing our dreams can lead us to a path of sorrow and isolation, instead of happiness and fulfillment.

The First Sight

It was love at first sight for Jack when he laid eyes on Ava. She was the most beautiful girl he had ever seen. Her long, flowing hair and sparkling green eyes had captivated him the moment he saw her.

They met at a local coffee shop, where Jack had been trying to gather the courage to talk to her for weeks. Finally, one day, he mustered up the nerve to strike up a conversation and ask her on a date. To his surprise and delight, she said yes.

They spent the next few weeks getting to know each other, and it quickly became clear that they were meant to be together. They had an undeniable connection, and their love for each other grew stronger with each passing day.

But their happiness was short-lived, as Ava's parents did not approve of their relationship. They wanted Ava to marry someone of a higher social status, and they forbid her from seeing Jack. Ava, being the obedient daughter she was, reluctantly ended things with Jack.

Heartbroken, Jack spent the next few months trying to move on. But he couldn't shake the feeling that Ava was the one for him. He knew that he had to fight for her, and he wasn't going to give up without a fight.

He decided to track down Ava's parents and convince them to let him be with their daughter. He spent months researching and planning, and finally, he had a solid plan in place.

Jack went to Ava's parents, and with all the charm and persuasion he could muster, he made his case for why he and Ava belonged together. To his surprise and relief, Ava's parents saw the truth in his words and gave their blessing for the couple to be together.

With the approval of Ava's parents, Jack and Ava were finally able to be together openly and without fear of disapproval. They built a happy life together, and it was all thanks to Jack's determination and the strength of their love at first sight.

Years passed and the couple grew old together but they never forgot that moment of the first sight, when their love story began. They were grateful for the challenges they faced early on in their relationship, as it made their love for each other even stronger.